REFLECTIONS ON DOMINION

A 14 DAY DEVOTIONAL

When God placed Adam in the garden of Eden, he gave him dominion over the land and the animals.

Has life got you beat and downtrodden?

Are you in despair and without hope?

Based on the book of Genesis 1:26-28, this is a 14-day devotional study reflecting on the

Power of dominion,

Walking in dominion

Rising to a place of dominion

Living in dominion

God is calling you to walk in dominion. Take this journey and experience one of God's original plan and design for humankind.

Rose Shiku

©Effective Global Training

1

ISBN: 978-0-578-90724-6

DAY ONE

DOMINION

Sovereignty, power, authority, or control

Genesis 1:26-27

[26] And God said, let us make man in our image, after our likeness: and let them have dominion over the fish of the sea, and over the fowl of the air, and over the cattle, and over all the earth, and over every creeping thing that creepeth upon the earth.

[27] So God created man in his own image, in the image of God created he him; male and female created he them.

Gratitude

Heavenly Father, I thank you that I am above and not beneath, the head and not the tail. (Deuteronomy 28:13) Thank you, Father, for giving me dominion and authority. Thank you because I am made in your own image.

4

God made man in his image and likeness. He then gave them the power and ability to walk in dominion and authority. Dominion is given to us; therefore, it is for us to exercise it daily. Understand and know that you already possess dominion.

Believe that you are above and not beneath (Deuteronomy 28:13)

Believe that you are the head and not the tail (Deuteronomy 28:13)

Do not yield to intimidation. Greater is he that is in you than he that is in the world (1 John 4:4)

Stand on God's word that he gave us dominion over all the earth (Genesis 1:26)

Pray from a position of dominion (Psalms 8:6)

Sovereign God, I humble myself before you. I thank you for the gift of dominion that you have graciously bestowed upon me. On this day, I arise in boldness and confidence, knowing that you have created me to walk and live in a place of power and authority. I arise to my purpose, full potential, and calling because you have placed me on higher ground, filled me with power, and adorned me with authority. Teach me to walk in dominion daily and to step over the enemy whenever he brings in doubt and intimidation. Give me the tenacity to rise to a position of authority when faced with setbacks and challenges. May I walk in dominion daily, and may I experience your power within me all my life.

In Jesus name

Amen

What areas in your life have left you feeling defeated?

_____

_____

_____

_____

Apply the word of God to every situation, speak to it from a place of dominion and authority.

Believe with all your heart that you are above this, confess daily, apply it daily.

What steps shall you make today to experience dominion in your life?

_____

_____

_____

_____

John 16:33 Be encouraged, you are an overcomer.

DAY TWO

Genesis 2:19-20

Now the LORD God had formed out of the ground all the wild animals and all the birds in the sky. He brought them to the man to see what he would name them; and whatever the man called each living creature, that was its name. [20] So the man gave names to all the livestock, the birds in the sky and all the wild animals.

Gratitude

Sovereign God, I thank you because you have given me the power and the liberty to use my words.

Job 22:28. (N.I.V)

What you decide on will be done

God gave Adam the authority to name the animals, and whatever he called them, God agreed. There is power in a name. There is power in addressing a thing, a situation, or a person by name. By naming the animals, he gave them an identity. What you name, you allow it to have an identity and a personality. What you name, you give it the power to exhibit character accordingly.

There is power in a name. God has given us the name above every other name, Jesus (Philippians 2:9-11).

Acts 3:6 Then Peter said, "Silver or gold I do not have, but what I do have I give you. In the name of Jesus Christ of Nazareth, walk."

God changed Abram to Abraham. Abram means exalted father and Abraham means father of many nations. (Genesis 17:4-6)

PRAYER

Almighty Father, you alone are great. You are the name above all names. I honor your name, for, in your name, there is power. Teach me today the power and authority in a name. Like Adam named the animals and what he called them, they became, may I know today that my words have power. As I put a name and a label to things, people, situations, circumstances, and events, they become so. Where I have named in a manner that is not according to your will, I pray for forgiveness. From today may my confession change and bring forth life to situations which I have spoken death over. May I walk in the knowledge of the magnitude and power in a name. Heavenly Father, may you honor that which I name.

In Jesus name

Amen

You have dominion and authority to name situations, events, and circumstances in your life. Despite what they look like we have the power to call those things that are not as though they are (Romans 4:17).

What labels have you given to situations and circumstances in your life?

_____

_____

_____

Give them a new name.

_____

_____

_____

_____

Genesis 17:5 God knew the strength in a name when he changed Abrahams name from Abram.

DAY THREE

BE FRUITFUL

Productive, successful, and fertile

Genesis 1:28

And God blessed them and said to them, be fruitful.

Gratitude

Heavenly Father, I thank you because in you I am like a tree planted by the river side, bearing fruit in all seasons. My leaf does not wither, my fruit does not dry up and whatever I do prospers. Psalms 1:3. Thank you for your constant supply of nourishment that keeps me fruitful.

God gave us a blessing to be fruitful. We become fruitful when we anchor ourselves in God, who is the nourishment that keeps us blossoming. How do we bear fruit? When our source is God, we look up to him when we are grounded and rooted in him daily. God's nourishment comes from a daily walk with him, a continual prayer life, fellowship with fellow believers, reading and meditating on the word of God.

When we are fruitful, we are fertile, we produce, and we are successful even when circumstances around us portray dryness. We flourish even when the world around us is perishing and withering. Life in God guarantees fruit in every season, situation, circumstance, and event. We have the divine ability in us to produce fruit in and out of season.

The earth is our ground for productivity. Maximize it as God intended.

Almighty God. I humbly come before you. I ground and root myself in you just like a tree planted by the riverside. I pray that I shall be like Isaac in Genesis 26 that even during a famine, I will flourish, I will be fruitful, and I will gain a hundred-fold as my harvest.

Almighty God fill me with the passion and desire to pray without ceasing. Give me the strength to read and meditate on your word. In receiving nourishment from you, I receive the grace and ability to bear fruit. Give me a hunger for your presence and the understanding that being fruitful comes with pruning. Give me a heart of obedience to go through pruning.

May I ever drink from the fountain that never runs dry, and as a result, I will never lack fruit.

In Jesus name

Amen

REFLECTION

Bearing fruit requires certain favorable conditions. In a world full of chaos and uncertainty, seek to be grounded in God so that you will be fruitful all round.

What situations and circumstances have dried up your fruit?

_____

_____

_____

What steps will you take to strengthen your roots in God?

_____

_____

_____

My trust is in you Lord therefore I will not fear the heat, my leaves remain green, and I will not be anxious in the year of drought. Jeremiah 17:7-8

DAY FOUR

MULTIPLY

Increase, enlarge, grow, and develop.

Genesis 1:28

And God blessed them and said to them, be fruitful and multiply.

Gratitude

I give thanks to you, Oh Lord, for the ability in me to increase, grow and multiply. Like the children of Israel, I will multiply and grow exceedingly strong Exodus 1:7. Thank you because there are no limits and glass ceilings to my growth, but multiplication in every area and aspect of my life is my portion. I multiply daily, and as I multiply, I become strong, resilient, and robust, rising above every limitation and constraint.

2 kings 4:1-7 A widow in severe debt cried out to Elisha for help and he instructed her to use what she had, a jar of oil. She gathered vessels as instructed by Elisha, and she began to pour the little oil she had into the jars she had collected. She sold the oil and was able to pay her debts and live on the rest.

With the power of God, the little we have can multiply. This woman exercised obedience by following the instructions of the man of God. A life of obedience unlocks a door for multiplication to manifest. Listen to the voice of God today and do as instructed. Live a life of obedience even when it does not make sense. The widow could have asked for an easier way out, but she chose obedience.

Multiplication adds to what you have. Look at what you have in your possession and allow the Lord to work with it and through it.

PRAYER

Elohim, you are the most high God. Power is in your hands to multiply. I pray today, take what I have, and multiply it. As you multiply it, may I head to your voice and purpose to walk in obedience. What you ask me to do, like the widow in 2 Kings 4, I will do. What you require of me, I shall fulfill. Touch my heart to be sensitive to your voice and your instructions.

I hold on to your promise of multiplication. It shall be added unto me as I seek your face (Mathew 6:33). I pray that I will not lack in any area of my life, but I will flow in multiplication. Heavenly Father, may you always remind me that it is not what I do not have, but what I have. May my eyes be forever open to see what I have.

In Jesus name

Amen

Sometimes in life we feel like we do not have enough to go around. Resources are scarce, supply is limited. What areas in life do you feel limited because you do not have enough?

_____

_____

_____

Like the widow in 2 Kings 4, what do you have?_____

_____

_____

As you seek God, listen to his instructions, write them down and purpose to walk in obedience.

_____

_____

_____

_____

Lord bless and multiply my womb, my land, my grain, my cattle, and my flock. Deuteronomy 7:13

DAY FIVE

FILL THE EARTH

Occupy, conquer, and inhabit.

Genesis 1:28

And God blessed them and said to them, be fruitful multiply, fill the earth.

Gratitude

Father, I express my gratitude today because you have given me liberty to occupy, conquer and fill the earth. Thank you because you have no limits, the earth is yours and the fullness thereof (Psalms 24:1). I am grateful because your word says that if I am willing and obedient I will enjoy the fruit of the land (Isaiah 1:19). Today I purpose to fill the earth and experience the best of it.

DEVOTION

To fill the earth means to occupy and to take charge. In Genesis 13:14-15, Abram was told by God to lift his eyes and look above. The first step was to refocus by lifting his eyes from his current vision. The next step was looking far and beyond because the Lord told him that as far as your eyes can see, I will give it to you. His vision was his possession. If he could see and visualize it, it was his. Refocus your sight, expand your vision to see more.

Next step Abram was told in verse 17 to arise and walk around the land. With this action, the Lord told him, I will give it to you. Make that bold step, make that decision, make that move. It was in Abrams walking around that he made possession of the land.

Fill the earth means experiencing the best of it all, the best that all God has for you, the best that the earth produces.

22

PRAYER

Heavenly Father, your word in Genesis 1:28 says that we should fill the earth. Today I pray, just like Abram, I will lift my eyes. I will shift my focus from all other distractions and lookup. I pray that my eyes will be open for me to see far and wide. Give me the vision to see beyond my limitations and shortcomings. I pray that just like Abram, I will walk around, I will not be stagnant. I will make the necessary move, the step, and the decision to walk around the earth because as I walk, I possess.

I pray that I will be willing and obedient so that I may eat the good of the land (Isaiah 1:19). I pray that I will have no limitations and nothing holding me back from your promise to occupy and fill the earth.

In Jesus name

Amen

REFLECTION

Are you constrained to one place and one thing? God has given us the freedom and liberty to fill the earth without restrictions.

_____

Expand your vision, refocus, and make bold steps in the direction you want to expand to.

Write down your vision and steps towards fulfilling that vision. You will go as far as what you can see.

_____
_____
_____
_____
_____

Joshua 1:3 that everywhere my feet shall step on, you have given me.

DAY SIX

SUBDUE

Overcome, subjugate, overpower, and control.

Genesis 1:28

And God blessed them and said to them, be fruitful, multiply, fill the earth and subdue it.

Gratitude

I thank you, Heavenly Father, because I arise over every circumstance and situation. Thank you because you have set me on high, and even when I am down, you lift me. I am forever grateful for your hand that upholds me through every danger, night, and storm. Because of your love, I dwell on high. Because of your grace, I soar like an eagle. Because of your Mercy, I prevail. Because of your faithfulness, I excel. I am an overcomer.

In the book of 2 Samuel, chapter 30:1-19 is the story of David and Ziklag. David and his men arrived at their camp in Ziklag to find their camp destroyed, burnt down, and all women and children had been taken captive. The bible says in verse 4 that they wept until they had no more strength in them. In verse 6, David's men turned against him and blamed him for the catastrophe.

After David wept, he got up and inquired of the Lord. The Lord's answer was yes, pursue, overtake, and you shall recover all. What had taken dominion over him, he went after it, subdued it, and got back all that had been stolen, including the women and children.

David did not dwell in his misery for a long time, nor did he allow the situation to overpower him. It was overwhelming for David, but he had the determination and faith that through the power of God, he would overcome.

PRAYER

I pray that when I am overwhelmed, you will lead me to the rock that is higher than I. (Psalms 61:2). A rock that cannot be shaken or moved. A solid and steady rock

Like David, I pray that I will always inquire of you when faced with an overwhelming situation. Give me the strength to rise and pursue just like David, without losing hope and giving up. There may be moments where I weep, moments where I cry, moments where people are after my life. In those moments, may I rise, dry my tears and seek help from you ruler above all, and may I find the strength to pursue, overtake and recover all.

In Jesus name

Amen

Do you feel like David, you have lost all and what you have has been destroyed? _____

Are you overwhelmed because the people that were with you are now against you? _____

What areas in your life do you need to bring before the Lord?

_____

_____

_____

Are you willing to take inquire of the Lord and take the necessary steps towards your victory?

_____

_____

_____

Listen to the Lord your God and He will subdue your enemies. Psalms 81:13-14

DAY SEVEN

RULE

Reign, take charge, govern, control.

Genesis 1:28

And God blessed them and said to them, be fruitful, multiply, fill the earth, subdue it and rule over the fish of the sea, the birds of the air and every living thing that moves upon the earth.

Gratitude

Sovereign God, I am grateful for the reign and charge that you have bestowed upon me. You have placed me power and authority on this earth, with everything in it positioned under my feet. Therefore, I rule, and I reign over your creation and the works of your hands.

DEVOTION

In the book of Acts 28:1-6, the Apostle Paul was shipwrecked on the Island of Malta. He was gathering wood to add to the fire, and a snake wrapped itself around his arm. The people of Malta were in shock and concluded that he must have been a murder, and now justice was being served. Paul shook his arm, and the snake fell into the fire. The people expected him to swell or drop dead, neither happened. When they say that, they stopped perceiving him as a murderer and now saw him as a god.

Paul knew he was on assignment, sent by God, and nothing would stop him. He knew the power within him to rule and reign over the serpents and scorpions, and no harm would come upon him (Luke 10:19). He had no fear; he stood firm; he was bold and confident even when all others around him were in fear.

PRAYER

Almighty, all-powerful God. You have placed in me the power and authority to rise above every situation. I refuse every form of fear and intimidation that hinders my walking in power and authority. By your power, you have set me on high places (Psalms 91:14 Amplified).

I pray that I will stand firm, unshakeable, unmovable. I pray for boldness to stand firm even when faced with adversity. Please give me the assurance and the confidence that you are with me, you care for me, and you are on my side.

I pray that people's (opinion of me) will not deter me or hold me back because I rule and reign in you.

In Jesus name

Amen

REFLECTION

What situations have you living in fear?

_____

_____

Do you feel intimidated by someone or something and why?

_____

_____

_____

What steps are you willing to take to walk in boldness so that you rule and reign in life?

_____

_____

_____

_____

Greater is he that is on the inside of me, than he that is in the world and everything that I see, hear, feel, or touch. 1 John 4:4

DAY EIGHT

WORK

Cultivate, tend, toil.

Genesis 2:15

So, the Lord God took the man and settled him in the garden of Eden to work it.

Gratitude

Heavenly Father, I thank you for the ability and the strength in my mind and in my body to work. Thank you for the wisdom you have put in me and the intellect to work. Thank you for the work opportunity and the inventive ideas to create work. For this, I am forever grateful.

For one to walk in dominion, work and effort are required. In the book of Genesis 26:1-32, Isaac was in Gerar, and there was a famine at that time. Isaac obeyed God's command to stay there. He became so wealthy that the Philistines told him that he was too powerful for them.

The Philistines then began to frustrate Isaacs's efforts. They started by filling up all the wells that Abraham, his father, had dug. They argued over every well that Isaac dug, and Isaac would proceed to dig another well. When Isaac dug the third well, they did not argue over it, and he said in verse 22, "The Lord has made room for us, and we shall thrive."

King Abimelech seeing that Isaac was unstoppable, came to make an oath and covenant with Isaac (verse 26-29) because he saw Isaacs's resilient efforts and God's mighty hand upon him.

PRAYER

Abba Father, my prayer today is to walk in obedience just like Isaac did. May I heed to your voice and follow your instructions. Where you lead me, I will follow, where you send me, I will go.

I pray that with the ability you have given me, I will put my hands to work. Please give me the strength, the willpower, and the intellect that I need to be a good worker. When I am weak, renew my strength like the eagle.

I pray for tenacity and persistence to not give up. Just like Isaac, even when my efforts are frustrated, I will rise, keep working, keep building, and keep going on because as I persist, I rise in dominion. I thank you, Lord, because all hard work yields a profit (Proverbs 14:23). And my labor is not in vain.

In Jesus name

Amen

Are you in a place where you feel your wells have been stopped up like Isaac?

_____

Are you going through frustration like Isaac where there is argument over the work of your hands?

_____

What steps can you take to make stand, be resilient, be persistent, and keep working?

_____
_____
_____
_____
_____
_____

The hand of the diligent rises to a place of rule and dominion. Proverbs 12:24

DAY NINE

WATCH

Take care of, keep in order, guard, observe.

Genesis 2:15

So, the Lord God took the man and settled him in the garden of Eden to work it and watch over it.

Gratitude

Father, I Thank you because you have placed me in a position of authority and put things under my care. Thank you for the capability to tend, take charge, and manage. You have filled me with wisdom and knowledge to govern. You have placed me in authority to guard and watch over the works of your hand. For this, I am forever grateful.

DEVOTION

To watch over and be on the alert means that you are aware and in control of your environment.

In 1 Samuel 17:34-36, David is a shepherd boy tending his father's sheep. He was always attentive, and when a lion or a bear took a sheep, he took control of the situation, rescued the sheep, and killed the animal. Being watchful gives you an advantage over the enemy or any distraction because you are alert and aware of your surroundings; hence you can take over the situation. When it came to facing Goliath, the giant, David had mastered the art of overcoming the enemy, so he feared not.

Being watchful over sheep put him in a position of power and dominion. He walked in it, and when an opportunity arose, he displayed it.

PRAYER

Great and mighty God. My prayer today is that my eyes will be open and alert to see the enemy's plans. I pray for spiritual alertness that I may discern the schemes of the enemy. Father give me an awareness of my environment and everything that concerns me. I pray that as I watch, I gain dominion and control over my territory. As I watch, nothing shall be stolen or taken away from me, and if so, I shall recover it.

I pray according to 1 Corinthians 16:13 that I will be watchful, standing firm, bold and robust. Father give me the ability, patience, and dedication to watch and to be alert. When my eyes get weary, renew my strength, and give me good vision and hindsight. Please help me to see not only what is near me but to see far and wide.

In Jesus name

Amen

REFLECTION

Do you feel like you have been watchful, but you are getting weary?

_____

Have you been overcome by situations because you were caught unaware?

_____

Purpose to be watchful, list the areas big and small that you need to keep your eyes on

_____

_____

_____

_____

Be on guard, be alert, be cautious because the enemy is roaming around looking for someone to devour. 1 Peter 5:8

DAY TEN

ADVERSITY TO DOMINION

Adversity is hardship, difficulty, misfortune.

Genesis 45:5, "I *am* Joseph your
brother, whom you sold into Egypt. [5] But now, do not
therefore be grieved or angry with yourselves because
you sold me here; for God sent me before you to
preserve life.

Gratitude

I thank you, my heavenly father, because
trouble does not last. Weeping may endure for a
night, but joy comes in the morning (Psalms 30:5). I
thank you because you see me through every setback
and every hardship. I will praise you through the rain
and the storm. In the night, I will worship you, and
in distress, I will exalt you. In you, I am an
overcomer.

Joseph was a man that faced adversity after adversity (Genesis chapters 37-45). He is hated by his brothers, who throw him in a pit. They later sell him as a slave in the land of Egypt. While a slave, his master throws him in prison after an incident where his wife accused him of attempted rape (Genesis 39:7-20).

Joseph, despite his circumstances, was diligent wherever life placed him. As a slave, he was given the master-slave position. In prison, the guards put him in charge. His character and gifts stood when he interpreted a dream for the baker and butler. When an opportunity arose to interpret a dream for Pharaoh, Joseph called to interpret.

In the presence of Pharaoh, his intellect, wisdom, character, gift, and faith in God were evident such that Pharaoh made him ruler and gave him the power to govern Egypt. Joseph rose from a place of adversity to a place of dominion.

PRAYER

Sovereign God. In a world of adversity, calamity, and hardships, you remain God. I pray that in the moment of adversity, you will rescue me. Even in hard times, may I exhibit my talents, gifts, and character that will set me apart and place me in a position of power and dominion.

Heavenly Father develop the gift within me. Please give me the zeal to nurture it and the wisdom to execute it. Shape and mold my character to one that is exceptional, trustworthy, and dependable. Let my faith and my speech be bold just like Joseph to speak before great men.

I pray that my gift will elevate me and propel me to higher heights.

In Jesus name

Amen

REFLECTION

Are you overwhelmed by situations that have brought hardships in your life?

_____

Do you feel like things are moving from worse to worse?

_____

Look within you, what gifts, and character can you display and lean on?

_____
_____
_____
_____
_____

Your gift will make a way for you and open doors for you in the presence of greatness. Proverbs 18:16

DAY ELEVEN

NOTHING TO DOMINION

Nothing means zero, unknown, nobody.

1 Samuel 16:13

Then Samuel took the horn of oil and anointed him in the midst of his brothers; and the Spirit of the LORD came upon David from that day forward.

Gratitude

Heavenly Father, I thank you because I am precious; I am your child and your beloved. Thank you for loving me just as I am. Thank you because you are shaping and molding me to a life of excellence, distinction, and prominence. With every new day, greatness is developed within me. Teach me, Oh Lord, your ways that I may never stray. May I forever hold on to your word and your unfailing love.

DEVOTION

1 Samuel, chapter 16:1-13, the prophet Samuel went to the house of Jesse to anoint the next king. Jesse had several sons that he presented before Samuel. With each son, even though they had the physical stature, God rejected them. David was the last choice, forgotten, and was not invited to this ceremony. Jesse not inviting David shows that he did not matter in the family and he was the least.

Samuel then sends for David. Verse 11 says, "for we shall not sit until he comes". David, who was a nobody in the family, was now the center of attraction. In Verse 12, God gives the assurance that David is the one. God was looking at the heart and not the physical stature (Verse 7). David's life changed from that day forward because the spirit of the Lord was upon him (verse 13). David, once a shepherd boy, became a king (2 Samuel 5:3). From insignificance to royalty. From being the least in the family to a place of authority

PRAYER

Almighty God, there is nothing too hard for you. By your power, you make things great. Through you, all things work together for good to them that love you. With you, nothing is impossible.

Today, I pray that you will create a clean heart in me and renew a right spirit within me, for you look at the heart and not the physical stature. Mold me and shape me to what you want me to be. The mortal man may forget me, despise me, and belittle me, but you, Oh Lord, have the power to raise me from nothing to dominion just like David.

I pray that you will bring me out to greater places at the appointed time, for your plans for me are for good and not for evil, to give me a future and a hope. In you, I am great. In you, I am destined for great things and great places.

In Jesus name

Amen

Has anything/anyone made you feel insignificant and forgotten?

_____

Do you feel lost in a big world with nothing to contribute to make an impact?

_____

David's heart touched God. Take inventory of the state your heart: what you need to embrace and what you need to let go?

_____

_____

Judges 6:15-16. I Gideon, come from the poorest clan and I am the least in my family, I have no ability to save Israel. But the Lord answered him that you shall smite them as one man, a mighty man of valor.

HUMBLE BEGINNING TO DOMINION

Esther 2:17

Now the king loved Esther more than all the *other* women, and she found favor and kindness with him more than all the [other] virgins, so that he set the royal crown on her head and made her queen in the place of Vashti.

Gratitude

Lord, I come before you with a grateful heart. Thanking you because your word says do not despise the day of humble beginnings. I thank you because you lead me to paths of greatness, and in you, I will rise to great heights. Thank you, Heavenly Father, because you do not turn away empty vessels, but you fill them up.

DEVOTION

Esther in Esther 2:7 was an orphan, and her uncle Mordecai took her under her care. She was fair and beautiful but had nothing much to her name. The time came when the King was looking for a new queen, so all the maidens were gathered and placed in the palace for one year of beauty treatment, and the King would pick one of them to be queen.

When her turn came to go into the King's chambers, the Bible says in Esther 2:17 that the King loved Esther more than all the other women. She won his approval, and Esther was crowned queen. Her life changed from a simple girl to queen, from nobody to prominence and dominion. She now had a voice, which she later used to save her people from being killed (2 kings 7:1-10). Even with a humble beginning, one can rise to a place of dominion through God's strategic and divine positioning. Esther, a girl with nothing much to her name, was now the most admired lady in the land.

PRAYER

Heavenly Father, greatness is ascribed to your name. Just like Esther, take me from one level to another, soaring to higher heights. Though my beginning may be small and J, through your power, elevate me to a place of dominance.

Begin a great work in me, for your word says that you are faithful to complete that which you have begun. Where I am today is a steppingstone of where you are leading me to. Please give me the patience to wait, the teachable spirit of learning, and the passion for holding on even when the journey is challenging. I pray that you will give me the revelation to understand that dominance is not about me but impact. Esther used her position of authority to save the lives of her people. May I emulate and walk-in her footsteps bringing liberation to many.

In Jesus name

Amen

Do you feel like there is nothing much to your name and you do not have much to bring to the table?

_____

Do you find yourself walking in fear intimidation?

_____

Believe that God can work with what you have and where you are to create greatness in you. What areas are you ready to release to God to do a work in you?

_____

_____

_____

_____

Job 8:7 Your beginning may be small, but you will greatly increase.

DAY THIRTEEN

TRIALS TO DOMINION

Tests, ordeal, distress, trouble

Daniel 6:25b-26

May your prosperity abound. I issue a decree that in all my royal dominion people must tremble in fear before the God of Daniel.

Gratitude

Almighty God, I bless your name because you are mighty and great. You command peace during a storm, and you make a roadway in the wilderness. You move mountains, you break the gates of brass and cut into pieces bars of iron. Even in the valley, you are still God because you bring me out. Your word says that even when I go through the waters, I will not drown, and when I go through the fire, I will not burn.

53

DEVOTION

In the book of Daniel 6, the administrators and satraps were trying to find a charge against Daniel. They found no wrong in him, and the only accusation they could bring was his faith in God. They got the King to sign a decree that no one should bow down to any other god except the King for thirty days. Failure to comply one was to be thrown into the lion's den.

Daniel was found praying and, as a result, was thrown into the lion's den. His faith was steadfast, and he did not compromise even when he knew the consequences. The bible says Daniel knelt and prayed three times as was his custom (verse 10). When the King saw that Daniel's God had saved him, he was overjoyed, and he gave a command that the people that had set up Daniel were to be thrown in the lion's den (Verse 24), and he declared that people must fear the God of Daniel (verse 26). Daniel prospered throughout the reign of King Darius and King Cyrus (verse 28)

PRAYER

Great and mighty God. You are sovereign above all. Great are the trials and tribulations that this world brings, but you are greater. Mighty are the storms of life, but in you is the authority to calm every storm. Even though I go through the valley of the shadow of death, you are with me.

I pray, just like Daniel, I will be steadfast in my faith and walk with you. Through every storm, every trial, I will hold on to your word and your promises. May I be consistent in prayer and communion with you. I pray that I will read and meditate on your word for you watch over your word to perform it (Jeremiah 1:12). I pray that even though I go through the fire, I will not be burned, and when I pass through the waters, I will not drown. Through your grace upon my life, may I triumph over every trial.

In Jesus name

Amen

Are you going through trials, are you distressed and has life been tough?

_____

_____

_____

_____

_____

Daniel was steadfast in his faith. Do you purpose to remain steadfast and in what ways will you purpose to do that?

_____

_____

_____

_____

God has promised the crown of life to those that stand firm in trials. James 1:12

DAY FOURTEEN

A LIFE OF DOMINION

Psalms 8:4-6

What is mankind that you are mindful of them? Human beings that you care for them? You have made them a little lower than the angels and crowned them with glory and honor. You have made them rulers over the works of your hands; you put everything under their feet.

To live in Dominion, one must understand that:

1. Dominion has been given to us (Genesis 1:26).
2. Dominion must be exercised and executed (Genesis 2:19-20)
3. Dominion is a daily lifestyle, walk in it, dwell in it. (1 Samuel 17:34-36)
4. Dominion comes with effort and hard work (Genesis 26:1-32)

5. Dominion is a part of Gods kingdom and is from generation to generation (Psalms 145:3)

Purpose to walk in dominion today. Is there an area in life, a person, a situation that has taken authority over you? Arise to a place of dominion by

1. Daily prayer for dominion
2. Daily declarations of dominion (Job 22:28 you shall declare a thing and it shall be established)
3. Walk in obedience (Deuteronomy 28:13, The Lord will make you the head and not the tail if you obey the commands of the Lord your God that I give you this day and carefully follow them, you will always be at the top and not the bottom)
4. Put on the full armor of God (Ephesians 6:10-17, put on the full armor of God so that you can take a stand against the devil's schemes)

PRAYER

All mighty and all-powerful God. I come before you with a grateful heart saying thank you because dominion has been given unto me. I pray that I will arise to a place of dominion, and dwell in that place. Today, I place all the cares of this world to you. Heavenly Father please give me the courage to navigate through them that they will not overcome and overwhelm me, but I will arise to a place of dominion where I am a victor and an overcomer. I stand on Genesis 1:26-28, I am made in your own image, in your likeness and you have given me rule and dominion over all the earth.

In Jesus name

Amen

CPSIA information can be obtained
at www.ICGtesting.com
Printed in the USA
BVHW020328190521
607639BV00006B/817